T0071052

Alan Bullard

A Light in the Stable

A cantata for Christmas

for SATB choir and organ or piano
with optional soloists, congregation, and with optional small orchestra
or chamber group

MUSIC DEPARTMENT

OXFORD
UNIVERSITY PRESS

Instrumentation

The work may be accompanied in three ways:

1. **With organ or piano**, using the accompaniment printed in the vocal score. The optional Small Bell (in the first movement only) may be played by any available musician.

2. **With chamber group**—1 Fl., 1 Ob., 1 Cl. in B flat/A, 1 Bsn. (or B. Cl.), 1 Tpt. in B flat, 1 Hn. in F (opt.), 1 Perc. (opt.) and 1 Hp. (opt.), together with keyboard (organ or piano). The keyboard part is not the same as that in the vocal score.

3. **With small orchestra**—all the instruments above with the exception of keyboard, together with either string quintet (2 violins, viola, cello, and double bass) or string orchestra.

Instrumental parts and full scores are available to hire from the publisher's Hire Library or appropriate agent.

OXFORD
UNIVERSITY PRESS
Great Clarendon Street, Oxford OX2 6DP, England

Oxford University Press is a department of the University of Oxford.
It furthers the University's aim of excellence in research, scholarship,
and education by publishing worldwide in the UK and in certain other countries

© Oxford University Press 2014

Alan Bullard has asserted his right under the Copyright, Designs
and Patents Act, 1988, to be identified as the Composer of this Work

All rights reserved. No part of this publication may be reproduced,
stored in a retrieval system, or transmitted, in any form or by any means,
without the prior permission in writing of Oxford University Press

Permission to perform this work in public
(except in the course of divine worship) should normally be obtained from
a local performing right licensing organization, unless the owner or the occupier
of the premises being used already holds a licence from such an organization.
Likewise, permission to make and exploit a recording of this work
should be obtained from a local mechanical copyright licensing organization

Enquiries concerning reproduction outside the scope of the above
should be directed to the Music Rights Department, Oxford University Press,
at music.permissions.uk@oup.com or at the address above

ISBN 978-0-19-340207-2

Printed in Great Britain on acid-free paper by
Halstan & Co. Ltd, Amersham, Bucks.

Contents

	Text	4
1.	Prologue: Of our Maker's love begotten	10
2.	The Journey	12
3.	As Joseph was a-walking	13
4.	The Shepherds	16
5.	Go tell it on the mountain | While shepherds watched	17
6.	The Angels	22
7.	Glory to God in the highest	22
8.	Hark! the herald-angels sing	28
9.	The Manger	32
10.	The Little Lord Jesus	32
11.	The shepherds visit the stable	35
12.	He is born (*Il est né*)	36
13.	Mary ponders these things in her heart	42
14.	Sing lullaby!	43
15.	The wise men	50
16.	As with gladness men of old	54
17.	The wise men offer their gifts	56
18.	A Light for Today	57
19.	Of our Maker's love begotten	59

Composer's note

A Light in the Stable is designed for church or concert use. The audience or congregation may join in the well-known carols in movements 5 (first verse only), 8, 16, and 19, as indicated, and optional readings are suggested.

The choir parts are designed with some flexibility in mind. They may be sung entirely by SATB choir, but movements 2, 4, 6, 9, 11, 13, and 17 may be sung by soloists, a semi-chorus, or all voices, as shown. Alternatively, these movements may be omitted and replaced by readings, as indicated. Movement 10 can be sung by upper voices (SA) or by SATB. In movements 5 and 14, and optionally in the final two pages of movement 19, there is a soprano part which may be taken either by a solo voice or by a semi-chorus from the main choir. Before the final movement there is a space for a reading and prayers, if desired.

The keyboard part may be played on piano or organ. Organists may wish to omit a few of the RH octave doublings, using the registration to thicken the texture. Pianists may omit the small notes in the LH or, where appropriate, play them in the RH, perhaps an octave higher. Alternatively, some chords may be spread.

Many of the movements can also be performed separately during the Christmas season.

Duration: *c.*35 minutes (without any additional prayers or readings).

Text

The Bible text is taken from the Authorized Version, and this is interspersed with new arrangements of traditional Christmas carols and hymns, and new settings of Christmas texts.

1. Prologue: Of our Maker's love begotten

1. Of our Maker's love begotten,
Ere the world began to be,
From Alpha to Omega,
Stretching to eternity.
Of the things that are, that have been,
And that future years shall see,
Evermore and evermore.

2. By your word was all created,
You commanded and 'twas done,
Earth and sky and boundless ocean,
Universe of Three in One.
All that sees the moon's soft radiance,
All that breathes beneath the sun,
Evermore and evermore.

Prudentius, trans. J. M. Neale, H. W. Baker, and R. F. Davis, altd.

2. The Journey

And it came to pass in those days, that there went out a decree from Caesar Augustus, that all the world should be taxed. And Joseph also went up from Galilee, out of the city of Nazareth, into Judaea, unto the city of David, which is called Bethlehem; to be taxed with Mary his espoused wife, being great with child.

Luke 2: 1, 4–5 (abridged)

As an alternative to this movement, a reading may be substituted, for example Luke 2: 1–5 (complete).

3. As Joseph was a-walking

1. As Joseph was a-walking,
He heard an angel sing:
'This night there shall be born
On earth our heav'nly King.'

2. 'He neither shall be born
In mansion nor in hall,
Nor in the place of Paradise,
But in an ox's stall.'

3. 'He neither shall be clothed
In purple nor in pall,
But all in fair linen
As wear babies all.'

4. 'He neither shall be rocked
In silver nor in gold,
But in a wooden cradle
That rocks upon the mould.'

5. As Joseph was a-walking,
He heard an angel sing:
'This night there shall be born
On earth our heav'nly King.'

As Joseph was a-walking.

English trad., altd.

4. The Shepherds

And there were in the same country shepherds abiding in the fields, keeping watch over their flock by night. And, lo, the angel of the Lord came upon them, and the glory of the Lord shone round about them: and they were sore afraid. And the angel said unto them:

Luke 2: 8–10a

As an alternative to this movement, a reading may be substituted, for example Luke 2: 8–12.

5. Go tell it on the mountain | While shepherds watched

Go tell it on the mountain
Over the hills and ev'rywhere,
Go tell it on the mountain
That Jesus Christ is born.

1. While shepherds kept their watching
O'er silent flocks by night,
Behold, throughout the heavens
There shone a glorious light.

Go tell it on the mountain (etc.)

2. The shepherds feared and trembled,
When lo, above the earth
Rang out the angel chorus
That hailed our Saviour's birth.

Go tell it on the mountain (etc.)

3. Down in a lonely manger
The humble Christ was born,
And God sent us salvation
That blessed Christmas morn.

Go tell it on the mountain
That Christ is born!

Trad., compiled by J. W. Work

1. While shepherds watched their flocks by night,
All seated on the ground,
The angel of the Lord came down,
And glory shone around.

2. 'Fear not,' said he (for mighty dread
Had seized their troubled mind);
'Glad tidings of great joy I bring
To you and all mankind.

3. 'To you in David's town this day
Is born of David's line
A Saviour, who is Christ the Lord;
And this shall be the sign:

4. 'The heav'nly Babe you there shall find
To human view displayed,
All meanly wrapped in swathing bands,
And in a manger laid.'

Nahum Tate, altd.

6. The Angels

And suddenly there was with the angel a multitude of the heav'nly host praising God, and saying:

Luke 2: 13

As an alternative to this movement, a reading may be substituted, e.g. Luke 2: 13–14.

7. Glory to God in the highest

Glory to God in the highest heav'ns, and on earth peace, goodwill toward all people.
Gloria in excelsis Deo!

Luke 2: 14, altd.

8. Hark! the herald-angels sing

1. Hark! the herald-angels sing
Glory to the new-born King;
Peace on earth and mercy mild,
God and sinners reconciled:
Joyful all ye nations rise,
Join the triumph of the skies,
With th'angelic host proclaim,
Christ is born in Bethlehem.
Hark! the herald-angels sing
Glory to the new-born King.

2. Christ, by highest heav'n adored,
Christ, the everlasting Lord,
Late in time behold him come
Offspring of a virgin's womb:
Veiled in flesh the Godhead see,
Hail th'incarnate Deity!
Pleased as man with us to dwell,
Jesus, our Emmanuel.
Hark! the herald-angels sing
Glory to the new-born King.

3. Hail the heav'n-born Prince of Peace!
Hail the Sun of Righteousness!
Light and life to all he brings,
Ris'n with healing in his wings;
Mild he lays his glory by,
Born that we no more may die,
Born to raise us from the earth,
Born to give us second birth.
Hark! the herald-angels sing
Glory to the new-born King.

Charles Wesley, altd.

9. The Manger

And Mary, having brought forth her first-born son, wrapped him in swaddling clothes, and laid him in a manger; because there was no room for them at the inn.

Luke 2: 7 (altd.)

As an alternative to this movement, a reading may be substituted, for example Luke 2: 7.

10. The Little Lord Jesus

1. Away in a manger, no crib for a bed,
The little Lord Jesus laid down his sweet head;
The stars in the bright sky looked down where he lay,
The little Lord Jesus asleep on the hay.

2. The cattle are lowing, the baby awakes,
But little Lord Jesus no crying he makes.
I love thee, Lord Jesus! Look down from the sky,
And stay by my side until morning is nigh.

3. Be near me, Lord Jesus; I ask thee to stay
Close by me for ever, and love me, I pray.
Bless all the dear children in thy tender care,
And fit us for heaven, to live with thee there.

19th-century American trad.

11. The shepherds visit the stable

And the shepherds said to one another: Let us now go even unto Bethlehem and see this thing which has come to pass. They found Mary, and Joseph, and the babe lying in a manger. And they glorified and praised God for all the things they had seen.

Luke 2: 15–16, 20 (abridged)

As an alternative to this movement, a reading may be substituted, for example Luke 2: 15–17, 20.

12. He is born (*Il est né*)

He is born, the holy child,
Bagpipers pipe, merry fiddlers play;
He is born, the holy child,
Jesus Christ, come to us today.

1. Countless centuries have passed
Since the prophets announced his coming,
Countless centuries have passed;
Now our Saviour is come at last.

He is born (etc.)

Il est né, le divin enfant,
Jouez hautbois, résonnez musettes;
Il est né, le divin enfant,
Chantons tous son avènement.

1. Depuis plus de quatre mille ans,
Nous le promettaient les prophètes,
Depuis plus de quatre mille ans,
Nous attendions cet heureux temps.

Il est né (etc.)

2. He is gentle, meek, and mild,
Perfect in grace, with radiant beauty,
He is gentle, meek, and mild;
Calmly sleeps the Holy Child.

He is born (etc.)

3. Cradled in a cattle stall,
Friendly beasts around him lowing;
Cradled in a cattle stall,
Precious gift of God to all.

He is born (etc.)

4. Heav'n and earth are joined in one
By this child of mighty power,
Heav'n and earth are joined in one;
Welcome to God's glorious Son!

He is born, the Son of God,
Bagpipers pipe, merry fiddlers play;
He is born, the Son of God,
Jesus Christ, come to us today!

2. Ah! qu'il est beau, qu'il est charmant,
Ah! que ses grâces sont parfaites!
Ah! qu'il est beau, qu'il est charmant,
Qu'il est doux, ce divin enfant!

Il est né (etc.)

3. Une étable est son logement,
Un peu de paille est sa couchette,
Une étable est son logement,
Pour un Dieu quel abaissement!

Il est né (etc.)

4. O Jésus, roi tout puissant,
Si petit enfant que vous êtes,
O Jésus, roi puissant,
Régnez sur nous entièrement!

Il est né, le divin enfant,
Jouez hautbois, résonnez musettes;
Il est né, le divin enfant,
Chantons tous son avènement!

French trad., trans. A.B.

13. Mary ponders these things in her heart

And all they that heard it wondered at those things that were told them by the shepherds. But Mary kept all these things, and pondered them in her heart.

Luke 2: 18–19

As an alternative to this movement, a reading may be substituted, for example Luke 2: 18–19.

14. Sing lullaby!

1. Sing lullaby!
Lullaby baby, now reclining,
Sing lullaby!
Hush, do not wake the Infant King.
Angels are watching, stars are shining
Over the place where he is lying:
Hush, do not wake the Infant King.

2. Sing lullaby!
Lullaby baby, now a-sleeping,
Sing lullaby!
Hush, do not wake the Infant King.
Soon will come sorrow with the morning,
Soon will come bitter grief and weeping:
Hush, do not wake the Infant King.

3. Sing lullaby!
Lullaby baby, now a-dozing,
Sing lullaby!
Hush, do not wake the Infant King.
Soon comes the cross, the nails, the piercing,
Then in the grave at last reposing:
Hush, do not wake the Infant King.

4. Sing lullaby!
Lullaby! is the babe awaking?
Sing lullaby!
Hush, do not wake the Infant King.
Dreaming of Easter, gladsome morning,
Conqu'ring death, its bondage breaking:
Hush, do not wake the Infant King.

Sabine Baring-Gould

15. The wise men

Behold, there came wise men from the east to Jerusalem, saying, 'Where is he that is born King of the Jews? for we have seen his star in the east, and are come to worship him.' When Herod the king had heard these things, he was troubled, and he said: 'Go and search diligently for the young child; and when ye have found him, bring me word again, that I may come and worship him also.' And the wise men, being warned of God in a dream that they should not return to Herod, they departed; and, lo, the star, which they saw in the east, went before them, till it came and stood over where the young child was. When they saw the star, they rejoiced with exceeding great joy.

Selected from Matthew 2: 1–3, 8–10, 12

16. As with gladness men of old

1. As with gladness men of old
Did the guiding star behold,
As with joy they hailed its light,
Leading onward, beaming bright,
So, most gracious God, may we
Evermore be led to thee.

2. As with joyful steps they sped
To that lowly manger-bed,
There to bend the knee before
Thee, whom heav'n and earth adore,
So may we with willing feet
Ever seek thy mercy-seat.

3. As they offered gifts most rare
At that manger plain and bare,
So may we with holy joy,
Pure, and free from sin's alloy,
All our costliest treasures bring,
Christ, to thee our heav'nly King.

4. Holy Jesus, ev'ry day
Keep us in the narrow way;
And, when earthly things are past,
Bring our ransomed souls at last
Where they need no star to guide,
Where no clouds thy glory hide.

5. In the heav'nly country bright
Need they no created light;
Thou its light, its joy, its crown,
Thou its sun which goes not down:
There for ever may we sing
Alleluias to our King.

William Chatterton Dix, altd.

17. The wise men offer their gifts

And when they were come into the house, they saw the young child with Mary his mother, and fell down, and worshipped him: and when they had opened their treasures, they presented unto him gifts; gold, and frankincense, and myrrh.

Matthew 2: 11

As an alternative to this movement, a reading may be substituted, for example Matthew 2: 11.

18. A Light for Today

1. A light in the stable, a light for today:
A heavenly marvel, this joyous birth;
The Son of God in a bed of hay,
The child, who on this sacred day
Brings a kingdom that stretches from heaven to earth.
A light in the stable so bare; a light for today.

2. The wise men's gifts lie at Jesus' feet:
The gold a tribute to a King,
The frankincense, with its odour sweet,
Drifts heav'nwards in the rising heat,
The myrrh for the body's burying.
A light in the stable so bare; a light for today.

3. And Mary wonders and bows her head,
And sits as still as a statue of stone;
Her heart is troubled yet comforted,
Remembering what the angel had said
Of an endless reign, and of David's throne.
A light in the stable so bare; a light for today.

from *Three Kings came a-riding,*
Henry Wadsworth Longfellow, altd.

19. Of our Maker's love begotten

1. Of our Maker's love begotten,
Ere the world began to be,
From Alpha to Omega,
Stretching to eternity.
Of the things that are, that have been,
And that future years shall see,
Evermore and evermore.

2. By your word was all created,
You commanded and 'twas done,
Earth and sky and boundless ocean,
Universe of Three in One.
All that sees the moon's soft radiance,
All that breathes beneath the sun,
Evermore and evermore.

3. O that time for ever blessed,
When the Virgin, full of grace,
Brought to birth our holy Saviour,
Light for all the human race.
And this babe, the world's Redeemer,
First revealed his sacred face,
Evermore and evermore.

4. You, the one of whom the prophets
Spoke in ages long gone by,
Now to all the earth revealed,
As your Name we glorify.
Shining now, the long-expected,
Let us loud hosannas cry,
Evermore and evermore.
(Noel, noel, for evermore!)

5. Sing, ye heights of heav'n, in praises,
Angels and archangels sing!
Wheresoever we are gathered,
Let our joyful anthems ring.
Ev'ry tongue your Name confessing,
Countless voices answering,
Evermore and evermore!
(Noel, noel, for evermore!)

Prudentius, trans. J. M. Neale, H. W. Baker,
and R. F. Davis, altd.

for Philip Brunelle and VocalEssence, Minneapolis, USA

A Light in the Stable

A cantata for Christmas

ALAN BULLARD

1. Prologue: Of our Maker's love begotten

Prudentius (348–*c.*410)
trans. J. M. Neale (1818–66), H. W. Baker (1821–77),
and R. F. Davis (1866–1937), altd.

DIVINUM MYSTERIUM
Melody from *Piae Cantiones* (1582)
arr. Alan Bullard

This work may be accompanied either by organ or piano alone, with optional Small Bell in the Prologue only (using this score), or by small orchestra or chamber group, as follows:
1 Fl., 1 Ob., 1 Cl. in B flat/A, 1 Bsn. (or B. Cl.), 1 Tpt. in B flat, 1 Hn. in F (opt.), 1 Perc. (opt.), and 1 Hp. (opt.), together with **either** string quintet, **or** string orchestra, **or** keyboard (organ or piano). The full score and set of parts (including keyboard) are available on hire from the Publisher's Hire Library or appropriate agent.

© Oxford University Press 2014

Printed in Great Britain

OXFORD UNIVERSITY PRESS, MUSIC DEPARTMENT, GREAT CLARENDON STREET, OXFORD OX2 6DP
The Moral Rights of the Composer have been asserted. Photocopying this copyright material is ILLEGAL.

9
p
unis.
Of the things that are, that have been, And that fu-ture years shall see, Ev-er-more and ev-er-more.
13
S./A. unis.
mp espress., following the accentuation of the words
mf
S. A.
By your word was all cre-at - ed, You com-mand-ed and 'twas done, Earth and
mp
T. B.
By your word was all cre-at - ed, You com-mand-ed and 'twas done,
(p)
17
unis.
mp
sky and bound-less o - cean, U-ni-verse of Three in One. All that sees the moon's soft ra -
mf
unis.
mp
Earth and sky and bound-less o - cean, U - ni-verse of Three in One. All that sees the moon's soft ra -

attacca

2. The Journey*

Luke 2: 1, 3–5 (abridged)

Freely and expressively ♩ = *c.*72

S./A. SOLO, SMALL GROUP, or TUTTI

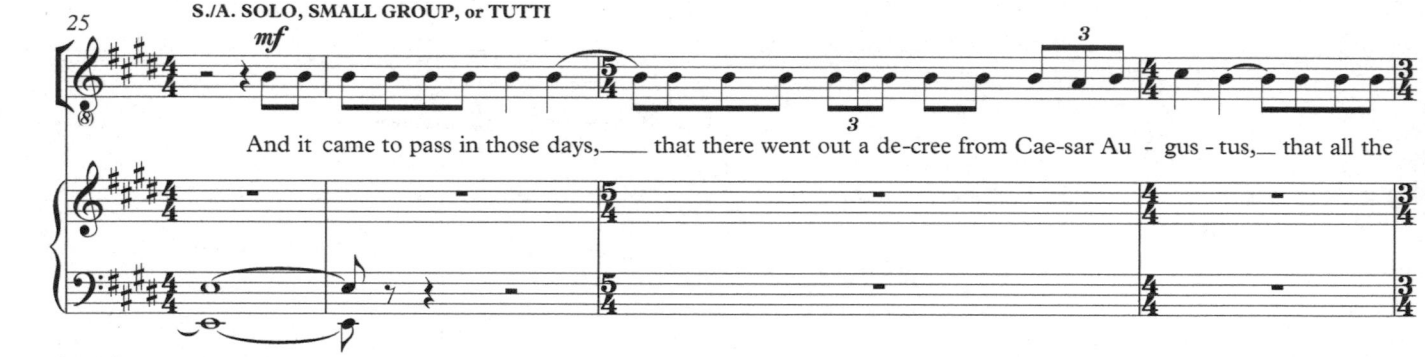

T./B. SOLO, SMALL GROUP, or TUTTI

A little slower

S./A. SOLO, SMALL GROUP, or TUTTI

attacca

* As an alternative to this movement, a reading may be substituted, for example Luke 2:1–5 (complete)

3. As Joseph was a-walking

English trad., altd.

Alan Bullard

60
p
Pa - ra - dise, But in an ox - 's stall.'
3. 'He
66
mp
nei - ther shall be clothed In pur - ple nor in pall, But all in fair lin - en As wear ba - bies
Man.
72
But in a wood-en
mp
all.'
But in a
4. 'He nei - ther shall be rocked In sil - ver nor in gold,
(Man.)
Ped.

* Some basses to sing low D, if possible

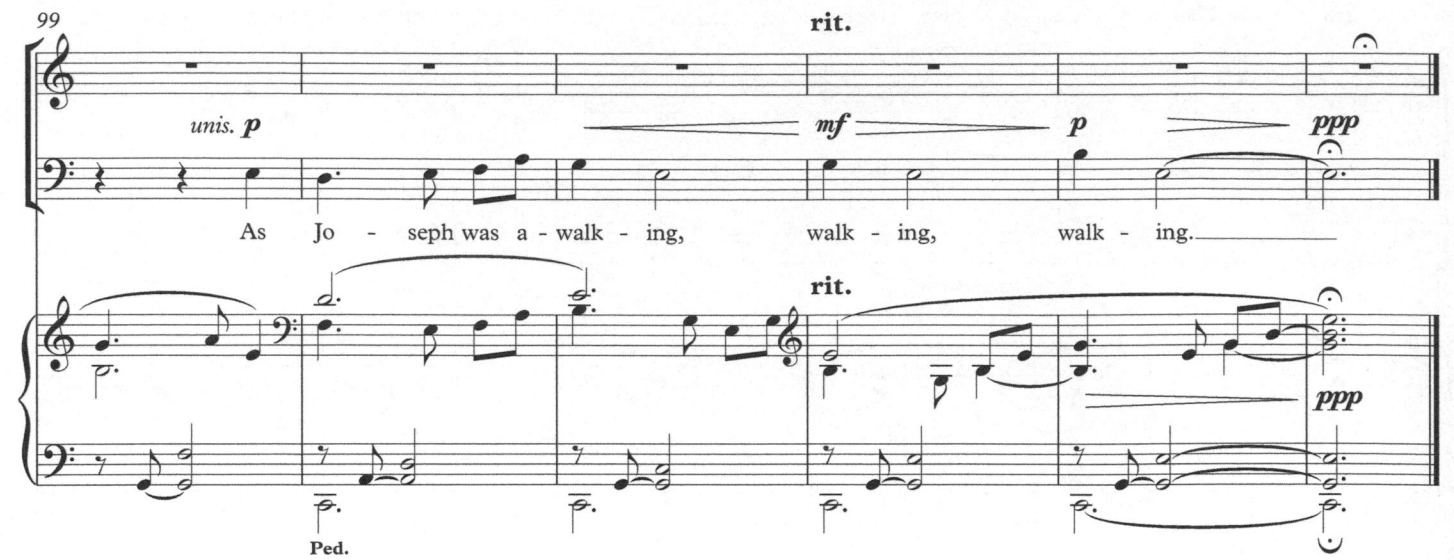

4. The Shepherds*

Luke 2: 8–10a

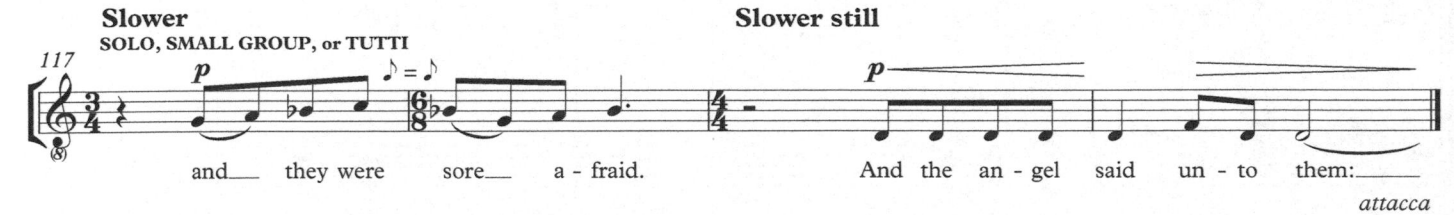

* As an alternative to this movement, a reading may be substituted, for example Luke 2: 8–12

5. Go tell it on the mountain | While shepherds watched

Trad., compiled by J. W. Work (1872–1925)
Nahum Tate (1652–1715) altd.

African-American Spiritual
WINCHESTER OLD, Este's *Whole Book of Psalms* (1592)
arr. Alan Bullard

Note: Audience / congregation sing (optionally) in verse 1 of 'While shepherds watched' only, seated

* *divisi* if sung by a group

158
rit.
A little slower ♩ = c.96
+ AUDIENCE / CONGREGATION in unison
mp
1. While shep - herds watched their flocks by night, All seat - ed on the
rit.
A little slower ♩ = c.96
mp
163
mf
And glo - ry shone a - round.
S.
A.
ground, The an - gel of the Lord came down, And glo - ry shone, and glo - ry shone a -
T.
B.
mf
And glo - ry shone a - round.
mf
AUDIENCE / CONGREGATION TACET
CHOIR S./A. unis.
168
f
2. 'Fear not,' said he (for migh - ty dread Had seized their trou-bled mind); 'Glad
-round.
CHOIR T./B. unis.
f
2. The shep - herds feared and trem - bled, When lo, a - bove the earth
f
Ped.

173
mp
ti - dings of great joy I bring To you and all man - kind.
3. 'To
Rang out the an - gel cho - rus That hailed our Sa - viour's birth.
mp
178
SOPRANO SOLO or SEMI-CHORUS
mp
mf
Go tell it on the moun - tain, O - ver the hills and ev - 'ry - where, Go tell it on the
S.
A.
mf
you in Da - vid's town this day Is born of Da - vid's line A Sa - viour, who is
T.
B.
mf
mp
mf
183
moun - tain That Je - sus Christ is born, is born.
p
unis.
Christ the Lord, And this shall be the sign:
4. 'The
unis.
p
p

* Small notes are an alternative option when sung by solo voice; semi-chorus should sing the lower part only

6. The Angels*

Luke 2: 13

With life ♩ = *c.*104

SOLO, SMALL GROUP, or TUTTI

mf 200 3 3 **TUTTI** *mf*

And sud - den - ly there was with the an - gel a

202 *f*

S. A.

mul - ti - tude, a mul - ti - tude of the heav'n-ly host prais-ing God, and say - ing:

T. B.

f

attacca

* As an alternative to this movement, a reading may be substituted, for example Luke 2: 13–14

7. Glory to God in the highest

Luke 2: 14, altd.

Alan Bullard

Fast – with joyful energy and precision ♩. = *c.*104

206

Glo - ry to God, glo - ry to God,

f

S. A.

Glo - ry to God,

f

T. B.

Glo - ry to God, glo-ry to God,

Fast – with joyful energy and precision ♩. = *c.*104

f

f

Man.

212
p
mp
mf
f
glo - ry to God, glo - ry to God, glo - ry to God, glo - ry to God, glo - ry to God, to
glo - ry to God, glo - ry to God, glo - ry to God, glo - ry to God, glo - ry to
218
ff
God, glo - ry to God, glo - ry to God, Glo - ri - a in ex - cel - sis De -
God, glo - ry, glo - ry to God, glo - ry to God, Glo - ri - a in ex - cel - sis De -
Ped.
222
-o! Glo - ry to God, glo - ry to God,
-o! Glo - ry to God, glo - ry to
poco a poco cresc.

228
mf
f
mf
glo - ry to God in the high - est heav'ns, Glo - ry to God,
mf
f
mf
God, glo - ry to God in the high - est heav'ns, Glo - ry to
f
mf
poco a poco cresc.
234
f
ff
glo - ry to God, glo-ry to God in the high - est, glo-ry to God in the high - est,
f
ff
God, glo - ry to God, glo-ry to God in the high - est, glo-ry to God on
ff
poco meno mosso ♩. = c.96
240
legato p
and on earth peace, peace, good - will to - ward all peo - ple,
legato p
high, on earth peace,
poco meno mosso ♩. = c.96
mf
pp
Man.

248
p
and on earth peace, peace, good - will to - ward all
p
256
mf
p
peo - ple, and on earth peace, good - will
mf
p
Ped.
Man.
rit.
263
p
and peace, to - ward all peo-ple.
p
rit.

272
Tempo primo ♩. = c.104
Tempo primo ♩. = c.104
pp
mp
(Man.)
279
p sempre
Glo - ry to God, glo - ry to God, glo - ry to God in the
p sempre
Glo - ry to God, glo - ry to God, glo - ry to
p sempre
Ped.
285
sub. f
high - est heav'ns, Glo - ry to God, glo - ry to God,
sub. f
God in the high - est heav'ns, Glo - ry to God, glo - ry to
sub. f

291
ff
Glo-ry to God in the high - est, glo-ry to God in the high - est, glo-ry to God, glo-ry to God,
ff
God, glo-ry to God in the high - est, glo-ry to God on high, glo-ry to God, glo-ry to
ff
297
fff
Glo - ri - a in ex - cel - sis, glo - ri - a in ex - cel - sis De - - o!
God, Glo - ri - a in ex-cel - sis,
fff
fff
303
fff
fff
Pno.: Ped.

attacca

8. Hark! the herald-angels sing

Charles Wesley (1707–88) altd.

MENDELSSOHN
Felix Mendelssohn (1809–47)
adap. William H. Cummings (1831–1915)
vv. 2 & 3 arr. Alan Bullard

328
Christ is born in Beth-le-hem. Hark! the he-rald-an-gels sing Glo-ry to the new-born King.
334
p
2. Christ, by high-est heav'n a-dored, Christ, the ev-er-last-ing Lord, Late in time be-
p
Solo
p
339
mf
-hold him come Off-spring of a vir-gin's womb: Veiled in flesh the God-head see,
mf
mf

344
f
Hail th'in - car - nate De - i - ty! Pleased as man with us to dwell, Je - sus, our Em -
f
f
349
-ma - nu - el. Hark! the he - rald - an - gels sing Glo - ry to the new - born King.
354
SOPRANO DESCANT
f
3. Hail the heav'n-born Prince of Peace! Hail the Sun of Right - eous - ness! Light and life to
ALL OTHER VOICES
f
3. Hail the heav'n - born Prince of Peace! Hail the Sun of Right-eous - ness! Light and life to
f

359
mf
all he brings, Ris'n with heal - ing in his wings; Mild he lays his glo - ry by,
all he brings, Ris'n with heal - ing in his wings; Mild he lays his glo - ry by,
364
f
Born that we no more may die, Born to raise us from the earth, Born to give us
Born that we no more may die, Born to raise us from the earth, Born to give us
369
tenuto
poco meno mosso
rall.
ff
se - cond birth. Hark! the he - rald - an - gels sing Glo - ry to the new - born King.
se - cond birth. Hark! the he - rald - an - gels sing Glo - ry to the new - born King.

9. The Manger*

Luke 2: 7, altd.

* As an alternative to this movement, a reading may be substituted, for example Luke 2: 7

10. The Little Lord Jesus†

19th-cent. American trad.

James R. Murray (1841–1905) (vv. 1 & 3)
W. J. Kirkpatrick (1838–1921) (vv. 2 & 3)
arr. Alan Bullard

382
Flowing, and not too slowly ♩ = c.96
S. or S./A. unis. or SOLO
p
1. A - way in a man - ger, no crib for a bed, The lit - tle Lord
A. or T./B. unis. or SOLO
Flowing, and not too slowly ♩ = c.96
p
Man.

389
S. (A.)
Je - sus laid down his sweet head; The stars in the bright sky looked down where he

† This movement may be sung by either SA or SATB

395
lay, The lit - tle Lord Je - sus a - sleep on the hay.
A. or T./B. unis. or SOLO
401
mp espress.
2. The cat - tle are low - ing, the ba - by a - wakes, But lit - tle Lord Je - sus no
mp sempre legato
Ped.
408
mf
cry - ing he makes. I love thee, Lord Je - sus! Look down from the sky, And stay by my
mf
415
p
side un - til morn - ing is nigh.
A. or T./B. unis. (TUTTI)
mp
3. Be near me, Lord
p
mp
Man.
Ped.

* Optional *divisi*; lower notes must be sung

11. The shepherds visit the stable*

Luke 2: 15–16, 20

* As an alternative to this movement, a reading may be substituted, for example Luke 2: 15–17, 20

12. He is born

(*Il est né*)

French trad., tr. A.B. *

French trad.
arr. Alan Bullard

* The original French words are provided as an alternative.

† *divin* pronounced *di-veen*

476
Since the pro-phets an-nounced his com-ing, Count-less cen-tu - ries have passed; Now our Sa-viour is come at
Nous le pro-met-taient les pro-phè-tes, De-puis plus de qua-tre mille ans, Nous at-ten-dions cet heu-reux
mf
481
mf
f
last.
He is born, the ho-ly child, Bag-pip-ers pipe, mer-ry
temps.
Il est né, le di-vin en-fant, Jou-ez haut-bois, ré-son-
mf
f
f
Ped.
486
fid-dl-ers play; He is born, the ho-ly child, Je-sus Christ, come to us to-day.
-nez mu-set-tes; Il est né, le di-vin en-fant, Chan-tons tous son a-vè-ne-ment.

2. He is gen - tle, meek, and mild, Per-fect in grace, with ra - diant beau - ty, He is gen - tle,
2. Ah! qu'il est beau, qu'il est char - mant, Ah! que ses grâ - ces sont par - fait - es! Ah! qu'il est beau, qu'il
491
p
ah
ah
ah
p
p
Man.
poco rit.
a tempo
meek, and mild; Calm - ly sleeps the Ho - ly Child.
est char - mant, Qu'il est doux, ce di-vin en - fant!
496
ah
poco rit.
a tempo
pp
501
pp
sub. f
He is born, the ho - ly child, Bag - pip-ers pipe, mer-ry fid-dl-ers play; He is born, the
Il est né, le di - vin en - fant, Jou - ez haut-bois, ré-son - nez mu - set - tes; Il est né, le di-
pp
sub. f
sub. f
Ped.

506
p molto legato
ho - ly child, Je - sus Christ, come to us to - day. 3. Cra - dled in a cat - tle stall,
-vin en - fant, Chan - tons tous son a - vè - ne - ment. 3. Une é - ta - ble est son loge - ment,
p molto legato
p
Man.
511
mp
Friend-ly beasts a - round him low - ing; Cra-dled in a cat - tle stall, Pre-cious gift of
Un peu de paille est sa cou - chet - te, Une é - ta - ble est son loge - ment, Pour un Dieu quel a -
mp
516
f
God to all.
-bais - se - ment!
He is born, the ho - ly child, Bag - pip-ers pipe, mer-ry
Il est né, le di - vin en - fant, Jou - ez haut - bois, ré - son -
f
mp
f

521
fid-dl-ers play; He is born, the ho-ly child, Je-sus Christ, come to us to-day.
-nez mu-set-tes; Il est né, le di-vin en-fant, Chan-tons tous son a-vè-ne-ment.
526
mf legato
f
4. Heav'n and earth are joined in one By this child of might-y pow-er, Heav'n and earth are joined in one;
4. O Jé-sus, roi tout puis-sant, Si pe-tit en-fant que vous ê-tes, O Jé-sus, roi tout puis-sant,
mf legato
f
opt. 8va
mf
f
Man.
Ped.
532
ff
Wel-come to God's glo-rious Son, glo-rious Son!
Ré-gnez sur nous en-tière-ment, en-tière-ment!
ff
ff

536
He is born, the Son of God, Bag - pip - ers pipe, mer - ry fid - dl - ers play;
Il est né, le di - vin en - fant, Jou - ez haut - bois, ré - son - nez mu - set - tes;
540
f
ff
He is born, the Son of God, Je - sus Christ, come to us, Je - sus Christ, come to us,
Il est né, le di - vin en - fant, Chan - tons, chan - tons tous, chan - tons, chan - tons tous,
pochiss. allargando
a tempo
544
fff
Je - sus Christ, come to us to - day!
chan - tons tous son a - vè - ne - ment!

13. Mary ponders these things in her heart*

Luke 2: 18–19

*As an alternative to this movement, a reading may be substituted, for example Luke 2: 18–19

14. Sing lullaby!

Sabine Baring-Gould (1834–1924) Alan Bullard

* In the *divisi* sections, Bass 2 may omit the small notes if necessary, joining Bass 1 on the upper notes

573
(✓)
p
shin - ing O - ver the place where he is ly - ing:
pp p pp
Hush, hush, hush, do not wake the In-fant
pp p pp
Ped.
578
mp
p
2. Sing lul - la - by! Lul - la-by ba-by, now a - sleep - ing, Sing lul - la-
p
King.
p
Man.

583
- by!
Soon will come sor - row,
Hush, hush, do not wake the In-fant King, do not wake the In-fant King, do not
Ped.
Man.
587
sor - row with the morn - ing, Soon will come bit-ter, bit-ter grief and weep - ing:
rit.
S.
A.
wake, do not wake, do not wake the In - fant King.
TENOR
T.
wake, do not wake, do not wake the In - fant King.
BASS
B.
wake, do not wake, do not wake the In - fant King.
rit.
Ped.

591
a tempo
pp
3. Sing lul - la - by! Lul - la-by
pp
p
pp
Hush, hush, hush, do not wake the In-fant King.
pp
p
pp
Hush, hush, hush, do not wake the In-fant King.
pp
p
pp
Hush, hush, hush, do not wake the In-fant King.
a tempo
Man.
595
sub. f
ba-by, now a-doz-ing, Sing lul - la - by!
Soon
S.
A.
pp
p
pp
p
Hush, hush, do not wake the In-fant King.
TENOR
T.
B.
BASS
pp
p
pp
p

600
pp relaxed
comes the cross, the nails, the pierc - ing, Then in the
f
Comes the cross, the nails, the pierc - ing,
f
opt. 8va
f
pp
603
rit.
a tempo
grave at last re - pos - ing:
pp
p
4. Sing lul - la - by! Lul - la-by,
pp p pp
p
Hush, hush, hush, do not wake the In-fant King.
pp p pp
p
rit.
a tempo
Ped.
Man.

609
pp
p
is the babe a - wak - ing? Sing lul - la - by! Dream -
pp p pp p
Hush, hush, do not wake the In-fant King.
pp p pp p
Solo
p
Ped.
614
f
- ing of Eas - ter, glad - some morn - ing, Con - qu'ring death, its bond - age
f
Dream - ing of Eas - ter, glad - some morn - ing, Con - qu'ring death, its bond-age
f
5
f

618
rit.
poco meno mosso
break - ing:
Hush, hush, do not wake the In-fant King.
Sing lul - la -
Man.
623
molto rit.
Hush, do not wake the In-fant King.
- by, sing lul - la - by.
- by, lul - la - by.
mm

15. The wise men

selected from Matthew 2: 1–3, 8–10, 12

Alan Bullard, based on fragments of *We Three Kings*, J.W. Hopkins (1820–91)

646
mp
ah
mf
star and are come to wor - ship him, wor - ship him.'
mf
seen his star and are come to wor - ship him, wor - ship him.'
mf
we have seen his star and are come to wor - ship him, wor - ship him.'
651
mp
S.
A.
ah
ah
unis. mf
T.
B.
When He-rod the king had heard these things, he was trou-bled, he was trou-bled,
mf
Ped.
658
mf
ah
ah
ah
f
and he said: 'Go and search di-li-gent-ly for the young child; and when ye have found him,
f

664
rit.
mf
p
ah
ah
ah
p
bring me word a-gain, that I may come and wor - ship him, wor - ship him al - so.'
rit.
p
671
meno mosso
unis. (or SOLO)
p
a tempo, but calmer at first
And the wise men, be-ing warned of God in a dream that they should not re-turn to
meno mosso
a tempo, but calmer at first
p
Man.
678
(TUTTI unis.)
p
mf
p
mf
He-rod, they de - part - ed; and, lo, the star, which they saw in the east, went be - fore them,
unis.
p
mf
p
mf
mf
p
mf
Ped.

687
S.
till it came and stood o-ver where the young child was. When they saw the star, they re-
A.
till it came and stood o-ver where the young child was. When they saw the star, they re-
T.
till it came and stood o-ver where the young child was. When they saw, when they saw the star,
B.
till it came and stood o-ver where the young child was. When they saw, when they saw the star,
f
ff
allargando poco a poco al fine
694
fff
-joiced, they re-joiced with ex-ceed-ing great joy, great joy.
-joiced, they re-joiced, they re-joiced with ex-ceed-ing great joy.
saw the star, they re-joiced with ex-ceed-ing great joy, great joy.
saw the star, they re-joiced, they re-joiced with ex-ceed-ing great joy.
(Ped.)
attacca

16. As with gladness men of old

DIX

William Chatterton Dix (1837–98) altd.

Abridged from a chorale, *Treuer Heiland,*
by C. Kocher (1786–1872), arr. Alan Bullard

723
earth a - dore, So may we with will - ing feet Ev - er seek thy mer - cy - seat.
souls at last Where they need no star to guide, Where no clouds thy glo - ry hide.
SOPRANO DESCANT
728
f
5. In the heav'n-ly coun-try bright Need they no cre - at - ed light; Thou its light, its joy, its crown,
ALL OTHER VOICES
f
5. In the heav'n-ly coun-try bright Need they no cre - at - ed light; Thou its light, its joy, its crown,
f
734
ff
poco rit.
Thou its sun which goes not down. There for ev - er may we sing Al - le - lu - ias to our King.
ff
Thou its sun which goes not down. There for ev - er may we sing Al - le - lu - ias to our King.
poco rit.
ff

17. The wise men offer their gifts*

Matthew 2: 11

* As an alternative to this movement, a reading may be substituted, for example Matthew 2: 11

18. A Light for Today

from *Three Kings came a-riding*
Henry Wadsworth Longfellow (1807–82) altd.

Alan Bullard, based on DIVINUM MYSTERIUM
Melody from *Piae Cantiones* (1582)

* Organ or piano may optionally double the choir throughout this movement

794
to a King,
f
mf
tri - bute to a King,
The frank - in - cense, with its o - dour sweet, Drifts heav'n - wards in the
tri - bute to a King,
f
mf
to a King,
803
bo - dy's bu - ry - ing.
p
pp
ris - ing heat, The myrrh for the bo - dy's, bo - dy's bu - ry - ing.
A light in the sta - ble so
A light in the sta - ble, a
p
pp
A light in the sta - ble
812
p
3. And Ma - ry won - ders and bows her
p
bare; a light for to - day.
pp
ah
light in the sta - ble so bare; a light for to - day.
pp
p
pp
bare; a light for to - day.
ah
head, And sits as still as a sta - tue of stone; Her heart is troub - led yet com - fort - ed, Re -
820
ah
ah
ah
ah

830

- mem - ber-ing what the an - gel had said Of an end - less reign, and of Da - vid's throne.

ah An end - less reign, and of Da - vid's, Da - vid's Da - vid's throne.

ah An end - less reign, and of Da - vid's, Da - vid's

838

A light in the sta - ble so bare;

f *p* *mf* *p* *pp*

rit.

throne. A light in the sta - ble, sta - ble so bare; a light, a light for to - day.

A light in the sta - ble so bare;

f *p* *mf* *p* *pp*

throne. A light in the sta - ble bare;

Optional READING, for example John 1: 1–14, and/or optional PRAYERS

19. Of our Maker's love begotten

Prudentius (348–*c.*410)
tr. J. M. Neale (1818–66), H. W. Baker (1821–77),
and R. F. Davis (1866–1937), altd.

DIVINUM MYSTERIUM
Melody from *Piae Cantiones* (1582)
and a fragment from *The First Nowell,* Anon. English,
arr. Alan Bullard

847

Joyful and dance-like ♩. = *c.*80

CHOIR + AUDIENCE / CONGREGATION in unison

f

1. Of our Mak-er's love be - got - ten,

f

Ped. *ad lib.*

* optional *divisi*

870
S.
A.
(ORG. or PNO.)
T.
B.
Earth and sky and bound-less o - cean, U - ni-verse of Three in One. All that sees the moon's soft
875
f
ra - diance, All that breathes be - neath the sun, Ev - er - more and ev - er - more.
f
S./A. unis. + CONGREGATION / AUDIENCE (upper voices only) in unison with S.
880
mp
3. O that time for ev - er bless - ed, When the Vir - gin, full of grace,
mp
(Man.)
885
unis.
cresc. poco a poco
Brought to birth our ho - ly Sa - viour, Light for all the hu - man race. And this babe, the world's Re-
cresc. poco a poco
Ped.

890
unis.
f
- deem - er, First re-vealed his sa - cred face, Ev - er-more and ev - er - more.
f
895
T./B. unis. + CONGREGATION / AUDIENCE (lower voices only) in unison with B.
T. B.
f
4. You, the one of whom the pro - phets Spoke in a - ges long gone by,
Solo
Man.
Ped.
900
S. A.
mf
S.
A.
No - el, no -
T. B.
(f)
Now to all the earth re - veal - ed, As your Name we glo - ri - fy. Shin - ing now, the long - ex -

905
f
ritenuto
-el for ev - er - more, and ev - er - more.
unis.
- pect - ed, Let us loud ho - san - nas cry, Ev - er-more and ev - er - more.
ritenuto
ff
poco meno mosso ♩. = c.76
911
optional SOPRANO SOLO or SEMI-CHORUS
ff
No - el, no - el,
S./A. unis. + CONGREGATION / AUDIENCE (upper voices only) in unison with A.
S. A.
ff
5. Sing, ye heights of heav'n, in prais - es, An-gels and arch - an - gels sing! Where-so-ev - er we are gath - ered,
TENOR
T.
ff
No - el, no - el, no - el,
BASS
B.
ff
No - el, no - el, no - el, no - el,
poco meno mosso ♩. = c.76
ff

917
no - el, no - el, No - el, no - el
Let our joy - ful an - thems ring. Ev - 'ry tongue your Name con - fess - ing, Count-less voi - ces
no - el, No - el, no - el for ev -
unis.
No - el, no - el for ev - er, ev -
molto allargando
a tempo
f
fff
922
for ev - er-more and ev - er - more!
ans - wer - ing, Ev - er-more and ev - er - more!
-er - more, and ev - er - more!
-er - more, and ev - er - more!
molto allargando
a tempo
fff